THE
FESTIVE FOOD
OF
ENGLAND

Henrietta Green

ILLUSTRATED BY SALLY MALTBY

KYLE CATHIE LIMITED

To Kate and Michelle, whose friendship
makes all things possible.

First published 1991 by
Kyle Cathie Limited
3 Vincent Square London SW1P 2LX

Copyright © 1991 by Henrietta Green
Illustrations copyright © 1991 by Sally Maltby

ISBN 1 85626 032 1

A CIP catalogue record for this book is available
from the British Library

Edited by Katrina Whone
Designed by Geoff Hayes
Printed and bound by Mandarin Offset

Contents

Shrove Tuesday

Before the Reformation, every Christian had to confess, or 'shrive', on Shrove Tuesday to prepare for Lent. The church bells would ring out throughout the country, summoning parishioners to make their 'shrifts' and even today bells are rung in Berwick-upon-Tweed in Northumberland and Scarborough in Yorkshire, where the Pancake Bell tolls at noon.

It was also the day when 'luxury' foods forbidden during Lent were eaten up. Meat was finished on the preceding 'Collop Monday', which left eggs, butter and fat, and these were invariably turned into pancakes. Although nowadays few people observe Lent, practically everyone eats pancakes on Shrove Tuesday.

Several villages hold pancake races. The oldest takes place at Olney in Buckinghamshire and is supposed to have started in the fifteenth century when an absentminded cook ran to church with her pancake pan sizzling away in her hand. The race is open to all women of the parish over sixteen who have lived within the boundaries for more than three months. They must wear a cap and apron and run the 415-yard course tossing their pancake at least three times. If they drop it, it goes without saying, they are disqualified.

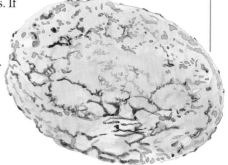

Simple Pancakes

makes 10–12 medium pancakes

This basic recipe can be either stuffed with a savoury filling or sweetened by adding 1tablespoon/1½tablespoons sugar to the batter and served with lemon or with jam or marmalade.

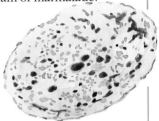

115g/4oz/1cup plain flour
pinch of salt
1 egg and 1 extra yolk
300ml/½pint/1¼cups milk
15g/½oz butter, melted
extra butter for frying

1 Sift the flour into a large bowl with the salt and make a well in the bottom. Beat together the egg, the egg yolk and 40ml/2tablespoons/3tablespoons of the milk, and pour into the well.

2 Using a wooden spoon slowly incorporate the flour into the egg mixture, adding the remaining milk a little at a time until the mixture is smooth and has the consistency of thick pouring cream.

3 Give the batter a thorough beating with a whisk while slowing adding the melted butter. Leave it to rest for at least one hour before cooking.

4 A well-greased, thick-bottomed pancake or omelette pan is essential for good pancakes. First heat the pan, wipe it with a little butter, then pour in about 20ml/1tablespoon/1½tablespoons of batter. Swirl it around the pan until it is spread evenly over the bottom in a very thin layer.

5 Cook for about 3 minutes, loosening the edges with a palette knife, and then, with a flick of the wrist, toss the pancake in the air, catching it uncooked side down. Cook it for another minute.

6 Turn it out and start again by greasing the pan . . . Keep the cooked pancakes warm in the oven, separated by a strip of greaseproof paper.

Stuffed Savoury Pancakes

Cook the pancakes as described above, and prepare the filling of your choice. Spoon 40ml/2tablespoons/3tablespoons of filling into the middle of each pancake, then roll them up loosely and place them side by side in an ovenproof dish. Scatter with grated cheese and heat either under a hot grill until brown and bubbling or bake in . preheated 180°C/350°F/gas4 oven for about 25 minutes.

Cabbage and dill filling
20ml/1tablespoon/
  1½tablespoons
  olive oil
30g/1oz butter
1 medium onion,
  finely chopped
450g/1lb cabbage,
  shredded
30g/1oz raisins
5ml/1teaspoon
  dill seeds
10ml/2teaspoons white
  wine vinegar
40ml/2tablespoons/3tablespoons single cream
salt and freshly ground pepper

1 Heat the oil and butter in a pan. Sweat the onion until soft, then add the cabbage, raisins and dill seeds.
2 Cover tightly, simmer for about 5 minutes then stir in the vinegar and cream and simmer for a further 3 minutes. You may need a little longer if you like your cabbage soft. Adjust the seasoning and proceed as above.

Leek, onion and thyme filling
20ml/1tablespoon/
  1½tablespoons olive oil
30g/1oz butter
350g/¾lb leeks, finely sliced
1 medium onion,
  finely sliced
3 tomatoes, skinned
  and chopped
2 sprigs of fresh thyme
40ml/2tablespoons/
  3tablespoons white wine
salt and freshly ground
  black pepper

1 Heat the oil and butter in a pan. Sweat the leek
and onion until soft, then add the tomatoes, thyme
and white wine.
2 Simmer for about 5–7 minutes. Adjust the
seasoning and proceed as above.

A Quire of Paper

These rich and very thin pancakes are piled one on
top of the other and eaten cut into slices, rather like
a cake. The recipe comes from *The Art of Cookery
made Plain and Easy* by Hannah Glasse written in
1747. They are made exactly as modern pancakes.

'Take a Pint of Cream, six Eggs, three spoonfuls of
fine Flour, three of Sack (sherry), one of Orange-
flower water, a little Sugar, and half a Nutmeg
grated, half a Pound of Melted Butter, almost cold;
mingle all well together, and butter the Pan for the
first Pancake; let them run as thin as possible: when
just coloured they are enough: And so do with all
the fine Pancakes.'

Mothering Sunday

The fourth Sunday in Lent, known as Mid-Lent, is also Mothering Sunday. In medieval times it was on this day that you travelled to the Mother Church or Cathedral to worship.

It was not until the mid-seventeenth century that it became closely linked to the family. From Lancashire to Devon every child living away from home – including servants and apprentices – would return bearing gifts and food.

Rather conveniently, Mothering Sunday is also Refreshment Sunday, the day when some relaxation of Lenten fasting is allowed. This is in honour of the Feeding of the Five Thousand, the Gospel reading of that day; so every family could feast with good conscience.

A favourite for Mothering Sunday was the Simnel cake. Its meaning comes either from the Latin *simnellus*, for the fine wheaten loaves baked on special occasions or from Anglo-Saxon *symel*, meaning a feast. Both explanations, it has to be said, are entirely appropriate.

Simnel Cake

Early Simnel cakes were much more like thin biscuity affairs than the rich fruit cakes that we eat now. They were always covered with almond paste or marzipan stamped with the figure of Christ and surrounded by twelve little marzipan balls to represent the twelve apostles. In some cases only eleven balls featured: Judas, it was felt by some, did not deserve a place.

Almond Paste
350g/12oz/2½cups icing or confectioner's sugar
350g/12oz/3cups ground almonds
3 large egg yolks
10ml/2teaspoons lemon juice
5ml/1teaspoon orange flower water
20ml/1tablespoon/1½tablespoons sherry

Cake
200g/7oz/1¾cups plain flour
55g/2oz/½cup rice flour
pinch of salt
10ml/2teaspoons mixed spice
pinch of baking powder
225g/8oz/1cup butter
225g/8oz/1cup soft brown sugar
4 eggs, separated
30g/1oz/¼cup ground almonds
20ml/1tablespoon/1½tablespoons dark rum
zest of 2 lemons
225g/8oz/1cup currants
115g/4oz/½cup sultanas
115g/4oz/½cup candied orange and lemon peel,
    finely chopped
40ml/2tablespoons/2½tablespoons apricot jam
20ml/1tablespoon/1½tablespoons water
1 egg yolk, beaten
icing or confectioner's sugar

1 First make the almond paste: sift the icing or confectioner's sugar into a bowl and add the almonds. Lightly beat the egg yolks with the lemon juice, orange flower water and sherry and pour into the bowl. Mix together and knead to a smooth paste. Wrap in greaseproof paper and keep in a cool place until you need it.

2 Preheat the oven to 180°C/350°F/gas4 and line a 20cm/8in round cake tin with well-buttered greaseproof paper.

3 Sift the flours into a bowl with the salt, spice and baking powder. Cream the butter and sugar until pale and fluffy, beat in the egg yolks one at a time, then add the almonds, rum and lemon zest. In a clean bowl whisk the egg whites into firm peaks.

4 Fold about one third of the flour into the creamed butter and then fold in the egg whites, alternating with the remaining flour, dried fruits and candied peel. Pour half the mixture into the prepared tin.

5 Roll one third of the marzipan into an 18cm/7in circle, lay it over the cake mixture and gently press it down. Cover with the remaining cake mixture.

6 Bake for 2 hours, then reduce the oven temperature to 150°C/300°F/gas 2, cover with two sheets of greaseproof paper and bake for a further 30 minutes or until a knife inserted into the cake comes out clean. Cool for about 15 minutes before turning it out on a wire rack.

7 To finish the cake, warm the apricot jam with the water and brush the top of the cake. Roll the remaining marzipan into a circle, lay it over the cake, trim neatly and make a criss-cross pattern with the back of a knife. Roll any marzipan scraps into twelve or eleven (depending on your convictions) small balls and place them around the edge at regular intervals. Brush with the egg yolk and put under a hot grill for a couple of minutes to colour. Serve lightly sprinkled with icing or confectioner's sugar.

Spiced Tea

serves 2–4

Spiced tea – yet another version of our national drink – was introduced by 'ex-pats' from India, who drank it by the gallon.

575ml/1 pint water
1 small cinnamon stick
8 cardamom pods
6 cloves
175ml/6fl oz milk
30ml/6teaspoons sugar or to taste
15ml/3teaspoons Indian tea

1 Put the water in a saucepan with the cinnamon, cardamom and cloves and gently bring to the boil. Cover and simmer for about 10 minutes.
2 Add the milk and sugar and simmer for a further 2 minutes. Then stir in the tea, cover and remove from the heat. Leave to infuse for a couple of minutes. Serve strained into teacups.

Good Friday

Good Friday – God's Friday – is the most solemn day in the Christian calender, commemorating the Crucifixion of Christ.

Numerous superstitions are associated with the day. At one time Devonians broke pieces of pottery in the belief that the sharp, jagged edges could cut the flesh of Judas the betrayer, whereas Liverpudlians burnt his effigy. In the Midlands it was the best day to plant crops; conversely, in the North and in Wales it was considered such a disaster to disturb the earth that people even walked barefoot to church. No clothes were ever washed in case the owner's life was washed away and for obvious reasons blacksmiths never made or hammered nails on Good Friday.

Originally made from the leftover dough of the sacramental loaves, hot cross buns are always marked with a cross in honour of our Lord.

Hot Cross Buns

15g/½oz dried yeast
55g/2oz/¼cup soft light brown sugar
200ml/7fl oz/¾cup milk, warmed to 80°F/28°C
450g/1lb/4cups strong white flour
pinch of salt
10ml/2teaspoons mixed spice
55g/2oz/¼cup butter
2 eggs, beaten
115g/4oz/½cup currants
shortcrust pastry trimmings (optional)
1 egg, beaten with water, for glaze

1 Sprinkle the yeast and 5ml/1teaspoon of the sugar onto 150ml/¼pint/⅔cup of the milk and whisk together. Leave in a warm place for about 10–15 minutes, until frothy.
2 Meanwhile, sift the flour into a large bowl with the salt, mixed spice and remaining sugar. Rub in the butter. Then add the yeast, the remaining milk and the eggs and mix together.
3 Knead into a soft dough, then scatter in the currants, kneading as you go to make sure they are evenly distributed. Cover and leave for about 1 hour in a warm place until it has almost doubled its bulk.
4 Have ready two lightly buttered bun trays dredged with flour. Knock back the dough and knead for a couple of minutes. Using a tablespoon fill each bun mould to about two thirds full, shaping the dough into a round ball. Leave in a warm place for 15 minutes to rise.
5 Brush the buns with glaze. To make the crosses either roll out the pastry, cut into long thin strips and lay them on top of the buns or simply make a deep cross-cut with the back of a knife.
6 Bake in a preheated 220°C/425°F/gas7 oven for about 15–20 minutes or until nicely browned. Cool on a wire rack.

St George's Day

The feast of St George, patron saint of England, falls on 23 April. Thought to have been a Christian centurion, he was martyred by the Roman emperor Diocletian at Lydda in Palestine around 303AD.

The famous legend of St George slaying the dragon is probably based on the Greek myth of Perseus's rescue of Andromeda from a sea monster.

It was not until Richard the Lionheart's crusade to the Holy Land between 1189–92 that St George acquired a special symbolic importance to England. When the king restored to Christian hands the church at Lydda containing St George's relics, St George was made patron saint of his army and to this day remains the patron saint of soldiers.

During the Middle Ages he became the embodiment of Christian chivalry. Knights wore his ensign – a red cross on white – on their tabards and shields and shouted his name as a battle cry. His cult grew when he was made patron of Edward III's Order of the Garter and in 1415 after the Battle of Agincourt, his feast day was declared as a national religious festival.

John Aubrey, the seventeenth-century diarist, was not convinced about St George's existence and wrote:

'To save a Mayd, St George the Dragon slew
A pretty tale, if all is told be true
Most say there are no Dragons: and tis sayd
There was no George;
Pray God there was a Mayd.'

Creamed Mushrooms

serves 4–6

St George's mushrooms (*Tricholoma gambosum*) are traditionally found on St George's Day and grow in grass on roadsides or wood edges. They have a good flavour but if you cannot pick or buy any do not despair; try this recipe with cultivated mushrooms spiked with a dash of Worcestershire sauce.

900g/2lb St George's mushrooms
55g/2oz/¼cup butter
5ml/1teaspoon lemon juice
150ml/¼pint/⅔cup double cream
40ml/2tablespoons/3tablespoons dry cider
salt and freshly ground pepper to taste

1 Carefully wash and dry the mushrooms, trimming the earthy parts from the stalks. If they are small leave them whole, otherwise slice them in half.
2 Melt the butter in a sauté pan and add the mushrooms. Sauté over a low heat for about 5 minutes, then stir in the lemon juice and half of the cream. Simmer for a further 5–7 minutes, season and remove from the pan.
3 Turn the heat up to full, pour in the cider and remaining cream and reduce to half. Pour over the mushrooms and serve immediately with sippets – pieces of toast.

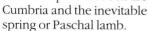

Easter

Eostre, or Eastre, the Saxon goddess of dawn, was worshipped at this time of year and the Saxon word *oster* means 'to rise' or 'to be re-born'. So it is not very difficult to see how the modern word for Easter was introduced into our language.

Several of the folk customs still popular at Easter are essentially pagan, dating back to the Anglo-Saxons – though they may since have acquired a Christian gloss. A Hare Pie Scramble takes place at Hallaton in Leicestershire and involves, as its name suggests, a pie that is first blessed by the Church and then 'scrambled' or fought over by the locals. This could be connected with the long-forgotten annual sacrifice to Eostra of a hare, a symbol of fertility; the 'scramble' stands for the fight between winter and summer as the earth struggles to awaken. Nowadays the celebrations are generally far less prosiac.

Easter is also the great excuse for a feast, particularly as it follows hard after the deprivations of Lent. There are sugar or painted eggs – the universal symbol of spring re-awakening; chocolate bunnies in just about every size and shape imaginable, cheesecakes from the Midlands, Easterledge Pudding made with bistort or 'passion dock' from Cumbria and the inevitable spring or Paschal lamb.

Lamb to Taste Like Vension

serves 4–6

Nothing beats a leg of new spring lamb roasted with sprigs of rosemary, slivers of garlic and served with a gravy made from its juices. Unfortunately, if Easter is early, it is rare to find new season's lamb and you are far more likely to be fobbed off with a piece of hogget – overwintered lamb – which is far less tender and sweet.

Faced with this option, the best way to tackle it is to marinate it as in this eighteenth-century recipe.

1 leg of lamb, weighing 1.35–1.8kg/3–4lb
20ml/1tablespoon/1½tablespoons olive oil
30g/1oz butter
3 medium carrots, sliced
3 medium onions, sliced
2 celery sticks, sliced
2 garlic cloves, chopped
575ml/1 pint/2½cups red wine
150ml/¼pint/⅔cup white wine vinegar
2 bay leaves
6–8 juniper berries, crushed
6–8 peppercorns, crushed
10ml/2teaspoons sea salt
sprig of fresh rosemary
sprig of fresh thyme
40ml/2tablespoons/3tablespoons finely chopped parsley
20ml/1tablespoon/1½tablespoons redcurrant jelly

1 With a sharp knife score the leg of lamb crossways into a diamond pattern, trimming away any loose bits of fat. Put the meat in a snugly fitting dish.

2 To make the marinade, heat the oil with the butter and sauté the carrots, onions, celery and garlic for about 5 minutes. Pour in the wine and vinegar, add the bay leaves, juniper berries, peppercorns and salt and bring to almost boiling point. Cover, turn down the heat and simmer for 15 minutes. Stir in the rosemary, thyme and parsley and leave to cool.

3 Pour the cold marinade over the lamb and leave it in a cool place for four days, turning and basting the meat twice a day.

4 To cook the lamb, first strain the vegetables from the marinade and scatter them on the bottom of an ovenproof dish. Drain the lamb and place it on top. Sear it in a preheated 230°C/450°F/gas8 oven for 15 minutes, reduce the heat to 180°C/350°F/gas4 and cook for another hour, basting occasionally with a little of the marinade liquid.

5 Allow the joint to rest for about 15 minutes before carving. To make the gravy, bring the remaining marinade liquid to the boil and reduce it by one third. Stir in the cooking juices from the lamb and the redcurrant jelly and reduce by another third. Adjust the seasoning and serve with the meat.

Buttered Carrots

serves 4–6
675g/1½lb carrots, cut into 6mm/¼in slices
55g/2oz/¼cup butter
5ml/1teaspoon sugar
20ml/1tablespoon/1½tablespoons finely chopped
  parsley
salt and freshly ground black pepper

1 Put the carrots in a saucepan with just enough
water to cover. Add the butter, sugar and a little salt
and bring to the boil.
2 Cook uncovered for about 10–15 minutes or until
the carrots are tender and the liquid has almost
disappeared. Season and sprinkle with parsley.

Paper Bag Potatoes

serves 4–6
Nicholas, grandson of the famous chef Alexis Soyer,
was also a keen cook. He developed 'Paper Bag
Cookery' and even wrote a whole book on the
subject. Based on the principle of sealing in the
flavour of the food, it is not as eccentric a method as
it may sound.

24 small new potatoes, scraped
4–6 fresh mint leaves
55g/2oz butter
large pinch of sea salt

1 Put the potatoes on a large sheet of greaseproof
paper with the mint leaves. Cut the butter into small
pieces, dot over the potatoes and sprinkle with the
salt. Fold the paper over, then fold the edges over
again, tucking them in so the bag is completely
sealed. Bake in a preheated 180°C/350°F/gas4 oven
for about 45 minutes.

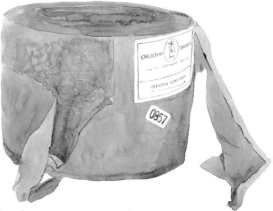

The Royal Bath and West Show

Every Cheddar cheesemaker will tell you that the show to win is the Royal Bath and West. Held annually at the showground in Shepton Mallet, the heart of Cheddar-making country, makers come from all over the world to exhibit their cheese.

'Benching Day', when the cheeses are laid out on benches ready for judging, is on the last bank holiday Monday of May. The judging takes place the following day when huge wheels of cheeseclothed farmhouse Cheddar weighing around 26kg/56lb are assessed on their body, flavour, texture, aroma, colour and finish.

Anyone who has eaten a good, matured farmhouse cheese will know that it should be a rich golden buttery yellow, firm to touch with a slight springiness and smell of new-mown hay. As for the taste, no cheese in the world can beat its rich, nutty flavour which gently kicks the back of your throat as you swallow.

Glamorgan Sausages

serves 4

These sausages are really a bit of a cheat as they do not contain a scrap of meat. Make them with any hard cheese that has plenty of flavour, such as Caerphilly or Lancashire or, of course, Cheddar, and serve as a first course or with a salad for lunch.

140g/5oz/2cups mature farmhouse Cheddar, grated
170g/6oz/2cups fresh white breadcrumbs
2 spring onions, finely sliced
3 egg yolks
20ml/1tablespoon/1½tablespoons finely chopped
 parsley
5ml/1teaspoon mustard powder
salt and freshly ground black pepper
1 egg white, beaten
oil for frying

1 In a large bowl mix the cheese with 140g/5oz/1¾cups of the breadcrumbs and the spring onions.
2 In a separate bowl whisk the egg yolks with the parsley, mustard, salt and pepper, and then mix this into the cheese mixture. You may need an extra egg yolk or a little water if it is too crumbly or dry.
3 Divide the mixture into 12 equal portions and roll each one into a small sausage about 5cm/2in long.
4 Dip the sausages in egg white and roll them in the remaining breadcrumbs. Heat the oil in a large frying-pan and fry the sausages until golden brown. Drain and serve.

Potted Cheese

Almost every traditional English cookery book includes at least one recipe for potted cheese and there are hundreds of versions – with or without walnuts, anchovies, cayenne and even sometimes with a pinch of sugar. Here one of Mrs Beeton's recipes has been adapted for modern-day machinery, as the food processor makes it unnecessary to pound by hand in a pestle and mortar.

225g/8oz/2½cups Cheddar cheese
225g/8oz/1cup butter
large pinch of ground mace
large pinch of mustard powder
large pinch of cayenne pepper
40ml/2tablespoons/3tablespoons dry sherry

1. Put all the ingredients in a food processor and blend until smooth.
2 Spoon the mixture into an earthenware jar, cover with greaseproof paper and store in a cool place. It will keep for several weeks but is ready to be eaten within a couple of days.

Welsh Rarebit

serves 4

This is another recipe that has endless variations – with or without beer, wine, mustard, eggs, flour, cayenne or Worcestershire sauce. In fact the only ingredients that are never in dispute are bread and cheese.

225g/8oz/2½ cups
 Cheddar cheese, grated
10ml/2teaspoons
 English mustard
75ml/5tablespoons
 light ale
pinch of cayenne
4 egg yolks
salt and freshly
 ground pepper
4 slices of buttered
 toast

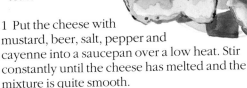

1 Put the cheese with mustard, beer, salt, pepper and cayenne into a saucepan over a low heat. Stir constantly until the cheese has melted and the mixture is quite smooth.

2 Remove from the heat and beat in the egg yolks, one at a time. Then return to the heat and continue stirring until the mixture thickens.

3 Have ready four slices of lightly buttered toast and spread them with the cheese mixture. Put them under a preheated grill for a couple of minutes until they start to bubble and turn a golden brown.

Blessing the Seas and Fisheries

All over England during Rogationtide – the three days preceding Ascension Day – agricultural communities have traditionally 'beat their bounds' when boundaries are fixed and crops blessed.

The piscatorial equivalent, held at the same time of year, blesses boats, nets and fisherfolk as well as the waters. The people pray for good catches and calm seas and each service is different, depending as much on local tradition as on the courage of the vicar. At Brixham in Devon, for example, the service blesses the entire fleet while it is safely anchored on the quayside, whereas at Mudeford in Hampshire the vicar is far more adventurous and actually puts out to sea. In Hastings a moored lifeboat doubles as a pulpit but in the Northumberland port of North Shields an entire choir plus vicar sail around the River Tyne.

Later on in the year there are also various thanksgiving Harvest of the Sea services when the churches are hung with fishing nets and the altar is decorated with fresh fish.

Fish Pie

serves 4–6

675g/1½lb mixed white fish, such as cod, whiting,
  hake or haddock
2 sprigs of parsley
1 bay leaf
50ml/3tablespoons/¼cup white wine
2–3 peppercorns
115g/4oz/½cup butter
30g/1oz/¼cup flour
300ml/½pint/1¼cups milk
900g/2lb potatoes, peeled and quartered
115g/4oz peeled prawns
1 onion, finely chopped
2 hardboiled eggs, sliced
salt and freshly ground black pepper

1 Poach the fish in enough water to cover, with the
parsley, bay leaf, 40ml/2tablespoons/3tablespoons
of the white wine, a pinch of salt and the whole
peppercorns for about 10–15 minutes. Drain the
fish, reserving the cooking liquor, remove any skin
and bones and flake it coarsely.
2 To make a white sauce, melt 30g/1oz of the
butter, stir in the flour and cook gently for 1 minute.
Measure 150ml/¼pint/⅔cup of the fish stock and
mix it with 150ml/ ¼pint/⅔cup of the milk. Add to
the pan, a little at a time, stirring vigorously the
whole time. Once all the liquid is incorporated,
simmer for about 5 minutes, stirring occasionally.
3 Meanwhile, boil the potatoes until soft, season
and mash with the rest of the butter and milk.
4 Arrange the fish in a buttered pie dish, and scatter
over the prawns, onion, hardboiled eggs and the
rest of the wine. Season the white sauce and pour
it in, then cover carefully with the potatoes.
5 Bake in a preheated 200 °C/400°F/gas6 oven for
30 minutes or until the potato is golden brown.

Sheep Shearing

'Wife, make us a dinner, spare flesh, neither corne,
Make wafer and cakes for our sheepe must be
  shorne;
At Sheepe shearing, neighbours none other things
  crave,
But good cheere and welcome like neighbours to
  have.'

The day sheep shearing began, a hefty dinner
would be laid on for the shearers and any friends,
neighbours or itinerant workers hired to help. Huge
trestle tables were set up in the farmyard for the
great quantities of farmhouse fare which would be
washed down with liberal amounts of ale, cider or
country wines; after a hard first day's shearing
everyone would relax and tuck in.

The farmers' wives of Yorkshire still have a fine
tradition of saucer cakes – pies baked in saucers –
and at this time they would make curd tarts because
milk was plentiful. Sometimes the tarts were even
made with beastings – the first milk from a cow that
has just calved – which made an extra rich filling.

Yorkshire Curd Tart

serves 4–6

Shortcrust pastry
225g/8oz/2cups plain flour
pinch of salt
115g/4oz/½cup butter
50ml/3tablespoons/¼cup cold water

Filling
115g/4oz/½cup butter
55g/2oz/¼cup sugar
115g/4oz/½cup curd cheese
55g/2oz/¼cup currants
grated zest of 1 lemon
pinch of salt
pinch of ground cinnamon
pinch of ground ginger
2 eggs, lightly beaten

1 To make the shortcrust pastry, sift the flour into a large bowl with the salt. Rub the butter into the flour with your fingertips until it has the texture of fine breadcrumbs. Add the water and work it in until the dough holds together; if it is still crumbly you may need a little more. Gather the pastry together into a ball, wrap it in plastic film and rest it in the fridge.
2 To make the filling, cream the butter with the sugar until light and fluffy. Beat the curd cheese into the mixture, then add the currants, lemon zest, salt, cinnamon and ginger. Stir in the eggs, giving the mixture a vigorous final beat.
3 Roll out the pastry to about 5mm/¼in thick and line a well-greased 20cm/8in tart tin. Prick the pastry all over with a fork and spoon in filling.
4 Bake in a preheated 190°C/375°F/gas5 oven for about 35 minutes or until the filling is set and has turned a golden brown.

Henley Regatta

Every summer for the last 150 years the Henley Regatta, one of the highlights of the Summer Social Season, has taken place. Held in the first week of July it turns the town upside down – during the rest of the year Henley, a prosperous town in Oxfordshire, is a quiet sleepy place.

Thousands of people flock to what is considered the longest and best straight stretch of the Thames. Picnicking and watching the races is for free from the towpath alongside the 1 ½ mile course; but anyone who is anyone will want to be seen in the Stewards' Enclosure. Inside, no one misses the opportunity to dress up, the ladies in hats and floaty frocks (even today no knees are allowed) and the men in blazers, boaters or caps trimmed with their old schools' rowing colours.

There are several trophies to be won for single sculls, pairs, coxed and coxless fours and eights. Between races there is plenty of time to socialize, to listen to the regimental bands, to consume copious quantities of Pimms and, of course, to picnic. The place to lunch is – believe it or not – in the Stewards' Car Park and reserved places are prized almost as highly as family portraits. These are no ordinary picnics – folding chairs and tables are set out next to the Rolls, Bentleys and BMWs, and a sumptuous spread is laid out and consumed amidst the family silver.

Veal, Pork and Chicken Pie

makes a 1.25kg/2¾lb pie

Strictly speaking, raised pies should be handmade around a 'dolly' or mould but, unless you have had plenty of practice, this can be rather tricky. It is far easier to use a hinged pie tin or a loose-bottomed cake tin.

Jelly
2 pig's trotters, split
1 veal knuckle
1 large onion, stuck with 2 cloves
3 medium carrots, left whole
1 bay leaf, 2–3 sprigs of parsley, 6–8 peppercorns

Hot Water Crust Pastry
450g/1lb/4cups plain white flour
5ml/1teaspoon salt
170g/6oz/¾cup lard
200ml/7fl oz water

Filling
170g/6oz lean veal, coarsely minced
285g/10oz lean pork, coarsely minced
225g/8oz pork fat, coarsely minced
20ml/1tablespoon/1½tablespoons chopped fresh thyme
2 garlic cloves, crushed
1 egg, lightly beaten
50ml/3tablespoons/¼cup dry sherry
large bunch of parsley, chopped
115g/4oz chicken breast, cut into strips
salt and freshly ground black pepper

1 First, to make the jelly, simmer all the ingredients together for at least 4 hours. Strain it and allow it to cool and set before skimming off the fat. If it is still a little runny, reduce it by boiling.

2 Meanwhile, make the pastry: sift the flour with the salt into a warm mixing bowl. Melt the lard in the water, bring to the boil and pour into the flour, mixing with a wooden spoon.

3 When the pastry is cool enough to handle, turn it out onto a floured surface and knead it for about 5 minutes or until smooth. Cover and leave in a warm place for 30 minutes to rest.

4 Divide the pastry into three and set aside one third for the lid. Roll out the rest to about 6mm/¼in thick and line a well-buttered 18–20cm/7–8in loose-bottomed cake tin with it so that it fits snugly around the base and hangs over at the top.

5 To make the filling mix together the veal, pork and pork fat, add the thyme, garlic, egg and sherry, stir and season to taste.

6 Spoon half the filling into the lined cake tin. Scatter half the parsley evenly on top, then arrange a layer of chicken, season and cover with the remaining parsley. Finish with the remaining filling so that it reaches the top of the tin.

7 Roll out the remaining third of pastry to make a lid and lay it over the top. Roll over the overhanging edges and pinch them together with the lid to seal them. Brush the top with water, add leaves cut from pastry trimmings and cut a steam hole.

8 Bake in a preheated 200°C/400°F/gas6 oven for 20 minutes, then lower the heat to 160°C/325°F/gas3 and continue baking for another 2 hours. Remove from the oven and let it stand for about 30 minutes. Remove the cake tin ring and return the pie to the oven for a further 15 minutes or until the sides turn a golden brown. If the top starts to catch, cover it with greaseproof paper.

9 Let the pie cool for about 20 minutes, then pour in the jelly through the steam hole – this is easier if you use a funnel – until you can see it through the hole. Leave it for at least two or three hours before you think of cutting it.

Summer Pudding

serves 8–10

Summer puddings are very transportable provided you do not turn them out until you arrive. Serve with lashings of thick cream kept in a portable cooler to prevent it from spoiling on a hot summer's day.

900g/2lb blackcurrants, redcurrants, white currants, raspberries, bilberries
115g/4oz/½cup sugar
20ml/1tablespoon/1½tablespoons blackcurrant cordial
40ml/2tablespoons/3tablespoons white wine
day-old white bread, crusts removed and cut into 5mm/ ¼in thick slices

1 Put the fruit with the sugar, blackcurrant cordial and white wine in a saucepan. Simmer gently for about 5 minutes or until the fruit softens slightly. Leave to cool.
2 Cut a circle from one slice of bread to fit the bottom of a 1.5litre/2 ½pint pudding basin. Then cut the rest into wedges to line the side of the basin. Every gap must be filled with bread; otherwise the pudding will not hold together.
3 Using a slotted spoon ladle the fruit into the bowl. Cover the top neatly with a couple of layers of bread. Pour over the juice, then place a plate on top and weight it with a couple of kitchen weights or heavy tins. Put it in the fridge and leave overnight, or longer.
4 To turn the pudding out, run a thin knife between the pudding and the basin, put a serving dish upside down on top and turn it over quickly, giving it a quick, sharp shake.

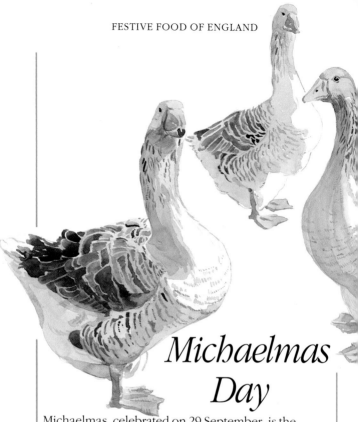

Michaelmas Day

Michaelmas, celebrated on 29 September, is the Feast Day of St Michael and All Angels. It is also Quarter Day or Martinmas, when landlords and tenants would fix and pay their rent and farm labourers went to the hiring fairs in search of work.

The best known of these fairs are still held in Tavistock, and in Devon and Nottingham. They were often known as Goose Fairs, as they would also be the occasion when the farmers would drive their geese to market. The birds would be at their prime at this time, plump and tender, having been 'a-stubbing' – let loose in the fields after harvest to feed on the stubble – and the feast day provided the ideal excuse for roasting a bird.

It is worth remembering the old superstition that blackberries should never be picked after Michaelmas Day as the Devil was supposed to have spat on the fruit to spite his rival.

Roast Goose

serves 6

1 fresh goose, weighing 4.5–5kg/10–11lb
675g/1½lb eating apples, cored and cut into
quarters
2 medium onions, cut into quarters
8 sage leaves, chopped
1 cinnamon stick, crumbled
150ml/¼pint/⅔cup dry cider
salt and freshly ground black pepper

1 Prick the skin of the goose with a fork and rub it all over with salt and pepper. Pull out any loose fat from the cavity.

2 Mix the apples with the onion, sage leaves, cinnamon, cider, and some salt and pepper. Leave to stand for about 10 minutes, then stuff the bird with it.

3 Place the goose on a rack, breast-side up, and put in a preheated 200°C/400°F/gas6 oven. After 15 minutes, turn the goose over so that it lies breast-side down and turn down the oven to 160°C/325°F/gas3. Allow 20 minutes per 450g/lb plus an extra 45 minutes when roasting a goose in this way; a 4.5kg/10lb goose will need about 4 hours. Although this method takes longer than breast-side-up roasting, it means that you need not baste the bird; but remember to turn it breast-side up for the last 90 minutes to brown it.

Apple Sauce

serves 8

This is quite a sharp sauce but it suits the richness of the goose.

450g/1lb cooking apples, peeled, cored and
  quartered
30g/1oz/1½tablespoons sugar
1 clove
grated zest of 1 orange
grated zest of 1 lemon
40ml/2tablespoons/3tablespoons water
30g/1oz butter
salt and freshly ground black pepper

1 Simmer the apples with the sugar, clove, orange and lemon zest and the water until it has reduced to a purée.
2 Beat in the butter, remove the clove and season.

Fennel Stuffing

serves 8

If you prefer to save the goose liver for a pâté or terrine, you can substitute chicken livers in this stuffing. It is far more effective if cooked separately from the goose.

20ml/1tablespoon/1½tablespoons
  goose fat
2 medium onions, chopped
1 garlic clove, chopped
goose liver and gizzard, roughly
  chopped (see above)
100ml/4fl oz/½cup red wine
1 egg, lightly beaten
170g/6oz/2cups breadcrumbs
225g/8oz fennel, blanched, drained and chopped
salt and freshly ground black pepper

1 Heat the fat and sauté the onion and garlic until soft. Add the liver and gizzard and cook for a couple of minutes before adding the red wine and removing from the heat.

2 Stir in the egg and 85g/3oz/1cup of the breadcrumbs and then add the fennel. Season to taste and mix thoroughly.

3 Spoon the stuffing into a buttered ovenproof dish. Moisten the remaining breadcrumbs with a little extra goose fat taken from the bird as it cooks and spread over the mixture. Bake uncovered in the oven with the goose for about 45 minutes.

Red Cabbage

serves 8

Red cabbage is often served with goose as the flavours complement each other so well. It is difficult to overcook red cabbage and it tastes even better cooked the day before and then reheated.

20ml/1tablespoon/1½tablespoons vegetable oil or goose fat
2 medium onions, sliced
1 large red cabbage, shredded
juice and grated zest of 1 orange
large pinch of ground cinnamon
55g/2oz/¼cup brown sugar
100ml/4fl oz/½cup white wine vinegar
salt and freshly ground black pepper

1 In a large saucepan heat the oil and sauté the onions until soft. Add the cabbage, the orange juice and zest, cinnamon, brown sugar and white wine vinegar. Stir thoroughly and season to taste.

2 Cover the pan tightly and simmer very slowly for about 1½ hours or until the cabbage is soft. You may need to add a little water if it becomes too dry, so check the pan occasionally.

Dr Johnson's Birthday

Doctor Samuel Johnson – 'Dictionary Johnson' – was born on 18 September in Lichfield, Staffordshire, and every year the mayor, accompanied by members of the Johnson Society and pupils of his old school, visits his birthplace and lays a wreath on his statue in the square.

A Johnson supper is held in the evening in the Guildhall, where his favourite foods are served – steak and kidney pudding followed by apple pie and cream.

Steak and Kidney Pudding

serves 6

Suet Pastry
450g/1lb/4cups self-raising flour
5ml/1teaspoon salt
225g/½lb/1½cups shredded suet
150ml/¼pint/⅔cup water

Filling
675g/1½lb stewing steak, trimmed
40ml/2tablespoons/3tablespoons plain flour
10ml/2teaspoons chopped fresh thyme
225g/½lb ox kidneys, trimmed
450ml/¾pint/1¾cups good beef stock
30ml/1½tablespoons/2tablespoons dark ale
10ml/2teaspoons chopped parsley
salt and freshly ground black pepper

1 Sift the flour with the salt into a mixing bowl, add the suet and mix together. Slowly pour in the water, a little at a time, mixing with a wooden spoon until the dough holds together.
2 Have ready a well-buttered 1kg/2¼lb pudding basin. Set aside one third of the pastry for the lid. Roll out the rest to about 1cm/½in thick, and line the basin with it so that it hangs over at the top.
3 To make the filling, cut the steak into strips of about 7.5 x 2.5cm/3 x 1in, beat them with a rolling pin and dip them in the flour seasoned with the thyme, salt and pepper. Cut the kidneys into pieces small enough to fit inside the strips of steak, then put some kidney on each strip and roll it up.
4 Put half of the meat rolls into the lined pudding basin. Mix the beef stock with the ale and pour over the meat (any leftover stock can be boiled up and reduced to serve as a gravy). Add the rest of the meat and sprinkle over the parsley. Roll out the reserved third of dough to make a lid and lay it on top. Trim the edges, moisten them with a little water and pinch together to seal the pudding. Cover with a piece of pleated foil and over this tie a cloth.
5 Stand the basin in a large saucepan containing enough water to come halfway up the bowl and steam gently for 3 hours. Check every so often that the pan has not dried out. Turn out the pudding onto a hot plate and serve.

Colchester Oyster Feast

Colchester 'native' oysters are thought to be the best in Britain. They were so highly prized by the Romans that they were exported by them, packed in seaweed and kept fresh in seawater.

The rights to the beds were granted to the Corporation of Colchester by Richard I in 1196, and they are still owned by them. Every year in September the mayor and his councillors officially open the oyster-dredging season. They travel to Brightlingsea, where they don full regalia and set sail to the oyster-fattening beds in Pyfleet. There the town clerk reads out a proclamation declaring that the rights have belonged 'since time beyond which memory runneth not to the contrary' to the city. Then they drink a loyal toast and the major lowers the first oyster dredge of the season and eats the first oyster to be brought up.

A month later, on 20 October, the Corporation holds an Oyster Feast in Colchester's Moot Hall, where as many as 15,000 oysters are eaten by the four hundred lucky guests.

Oyster Soup

serves 6
24 oysters
55g/2oz/¼cup butter
2 medium onions, chopped
55g/2oz/½cup flour
100ml/4fl oz/½cup dry white wine
850ml/1½pints/3¾cups fish stock
dash of Tabasco
pinch of cayenne pepper
150ml/¼pint/⅔cup double cream
10ml/2teaspoons lemon juice
40ml/2tablespoons/3tablespoons chopped parsley
salt and freshly ground black pepper

1 To open oysters, first wrap your left hand – if you
are right-handed – in a cloth to protect your hand in
case the knife slips and to ensure a better grip.
Hold the oyster flat-side up in your left hand and at
the hinge end insert the oyster knife. Slide the blade
between the two shells and prise them apart. Once
it is opened, taking care not spill the juices, use the
knife to separate the flesh from the shell; then tip
the contents into a sieve placed over a bowl.
2 Heat the butter and sauté the onions until soft and
golden. Add the flour and stir in 40ml/2tablespoons/
3tablespoons of the strained oyster juices. Cook
gently for about 1 minute. Then add the rest of the
juices, the white wine, fish stock, Tabasco and
cayenne. Cover and simmer for about 20 minutes.
3 Add the oysters, cream, lemon juice and parsley,
and season to taste. Simmer for a couple of minutes
and serve immediately.

Harvest Home

The Harvest or Horkey Supper was once a rumbustious affair where events would get a little out of hand and, according to one country diary, thoughtful farmers 'laid clean, loose straw outside the barn, for those farm labourers requiring temporary rest and meditation'. By the beginning of Queen Victoria's reign it was probably no more than an excuse to get rip-roaringly drunk, a state of affairs thoroughly disapproved of by middle-class moralists. It must have been a great relief when in the 1840s two West Country rectors came up with the idea of a Harvest Festival service followed by a tea.

It soon caught on; all over the country altars were laden with sheaths of corn, baskets of fruit or vegetables, hymns were lustily sung, prayers were enthusiastically offered up in grateful thanks, cakes were baked, tea urns were heated and the farm labourers were kept strictly under control.

Harvest Bread

makes 1 loaf

The last sheaf to be cut from the field was highly prized as it was thought that the harvest spirit retreated there. It was usually plaited and made into a corn dolly but sometimes the corn would be specially threshed and milled for the harvest loaf.

30g/1oz fresh yeast
300ml/½pint/1¼cups warm water
675g/1½lb/6cups 85% wholewheat flour
5ml/1teaspoon sea salt
30g/1oz butter
150ml/¼pint/⅔cup water
1 egg, lightly beaten
30g/1oz poppy seeds

1 Mix the yeast into the warm water. Stir and leave for about 10 minutes or until it is frothy.
2 Sift the flour into a large bowl with the salt. Rub the butter into the flour with your fingertips until it has the texture of fine breadcrumbs. Add the yeast mixture and the cold water and mix to a soft dough.
3 Turn the dough out onto a floured surface and knead for about 5 minutes. Cover with a clean cloth and leave in a warm place for about 45 minutes or until the dough has doubled in size.
4 Turn it out onto a floured surface and knead it again, this time for about 10 minutes. Then roll into an oblong at least 30cm/12in wide and cut it lengthways into three. Pinch the strips together at the top, plait them and pinch them together at the bottom. Seal both ends with a little water.
5 Place the bread on a well-greased baking sheet, cover and leave in a warm place for 30 minutes or until doubled in size. Glaze the loaf with the egg and scatter the poppy seeds on top. Bake in a pre-heated 220°C/425°F/gas7 oven for 40 minutes.

Guy Fawkes

Early in the morning of 5 November 1605 Guy Fawkes, a Catholic, was discovered in the cellars of the Houses of Parliament. Hidden with him were barrels of gunpowder that he had planned to ignite later that day when the Protestant King James I was opening Parliament. With one almighty explosion the entire government of England would have been destroyed, leaving the way clear for the Roman Catholics to assume power.

The plot may have been foiled but Guy Fawkes has never been forgotten. Every year bonfires, piled high and topped with his effigy, are lit and fireworks illuminate the skies. For several days beforehand, kids wheel hastily constructed guys around the streets, collecting firework money and repeating the old begging rhyme:

Please to remember the fifth of November
Gunpowder, treason and plot!
I see no reason why gunpowder treason
Should ever be forgot.

Yorkshire Parkin

Parkin is eaten on Bonfire Night. As it improves with keeping, remember to make it well in advance and to never even attempt to cut it for at least a couple of days as it is far too sticky.

350g/12oz/2¼cups medium oatmeal
170g/6oz/1½cups plain flour
pinch of salt
30g/1oz/1½tablespoons sugar
large pinch of ground ginger
large pinch of ground nutmeg
large pinch of ground mace
225g/8oz/¾cup black treacle
115g/4oz/½cup butter
75ml/5tablespoons/⅓cup milk
5ml/1teaspoon bicarbonate of soda
30g/1oz/¼cup flaked almonds (optional)

1 Mix the oatmeal, flour, salt, sugar and spices in a bowl.
2 Gently warm the treacle with the butter without allowing it to get too hot. In a separate pan heat the milk to blood temperature and add the soda.
3 Pour both liquids into the oatmeal mixture and stir well. Grease and line with greaseproof paper a roasting tin and pour in the mixture.
4 Bake in a preheated 180°C/350°F/gas4 oven for about 40 minutes or until the parkin is firm to touch. If you like, scatter the almonds over the top after it has cooked for 15 minutes.

Shooting Lunch

The shooting season starts with the Glorious 12th in August, when grouse come under fire. On 1 September partridge, mallard, widgeon and teal come into season and from 1 October pheasant and woodcock are fair game.

The Edwardian aristocracy were famous for their shooting parties, when thousands of birds would be 'peppered with shot' and brought down during a single day's sport. They were thoroughly organized affairs employing the services of beaters to drive the birds into the path of the guns and loaders to make sure that both guns were ready to fire.

Very few women actually shot. Some would walk the shoot, but far more likely they would stay indoors sewing, reading or gossiping and only join the gentlemen for luncheon. Weather permitting, this was an elaborate affair laid out in the open air on trestle tables. Everything – the food, drink, linen, cutlery, china, glass and servants – had to be transported from the house by pony and trap, while the houseparty travelled in splendour in that modern invention – the motor car.

Mulligatawny Soup

serves 4–6

Brought to England by the British Raj, mulligatawny, meaning 'pepper water', is hot and fiery and just the thing to warm you up on an autumn day.

large pinch of cumin seeds
large pinch of coriander seeds
large pinch of cardamom pods
6 peppercorns
1 garlic clove
grated zest and juice of 1 lemon
1 bay leaf
1.5litres/2½pints/6cups beef stock
225g/½lb minced beef
2 egg whites, lightly beaten
40ml/2tablespoons/3tablespoons
  Madeira
55g/2oz cooked rice
salt and freshly ground black pepper

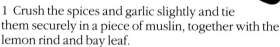

1 Crush the spices and garlic slightly and tie them securely in a piece of muslin, together with the lemon rind and bay leaf.

2 Put the spice bag into the stock, bring to the boil, cover and simmer for about 40 minutes to allow the spices to infuse. Remove the bag and let the broth cool.

3 To clarify the broth, skim off any fat and add the minced beef and egg whites. Whisk constantly as it comes to the boil, then leave to boil for 2–3 minutes. Turn down the heat, simmer for about 30 minutes and strain through a sieve lined with cheesecloth.

4 Add the Madeira, lemon juice and rice and adjust the seasoning.

Piccalilli

The Edwardians were very fond of their chutneys and pickles, which were always taken with a cold collation of cuts of beef, tongue or ham.

450g/1lb green tomatoes, sliced
450g/1lb green beans, sliced
450g/1lb carrots, sliced
1 cauliflower, cut into florets
450g/1lb pickling onions, peeled
225g/8oz/1cup salt
3.6litres/6pints/15cups water
50ml/3tablespoons/¼cup mustard powder
50ml/3tablespoons/¼cup ground ginger
20ml/1tablespoon/1½tablespoons ground turmeric
5ml/1teaspoon celery seed
115g/4oz/½cup sugar
1.1litre/2pints/5cups white wine vinegar
30g/1oz/1½tablespoons cornflour

1 Put the vegetables into a large bowl, and add the salt and water. Stir thoroughly and weight the vegetables so they are immersed in the water. Leave to soak in a cool place overnight.
2 Heat the spices, sugar and 1litre/1¾pints/4½cups of the vinegar in a saucepan, and simmer, stirring occasionally, for about 5 minutes.

3 Rinse the vegetables and add them to the pan. Bring to the boil and simmer for about 15 minutes or until they are soft but still a little crunchy. Strain the vegetables, reserving the cooking liquid, and pack them quite tightly into warm sterilized jars.

4 Stir the cornflour into the remaining vinegar and add it to the cooking liquid. Bring to the boil and cook for a few minutes, stirring constantly until it has thickened.

5 Pour it over the vegetables in the jars, leave to cool and then seal. Keep it for at least 6 weeks before eating to allow the flavours to mellow.

Potted Salmon

serves 4

Fish paste, a corrupted form of potted fish, is one of those extraordinary British inventions that understandably enough no other country has adopted with any enthusiasm.

Properly done, potted preparations are excellent; potting was the old-fashioned technique of pounding meat, cheese, game or fish, or a mixture, with spices and butter, then sealing them in a jar with a layer of butter or lard to act as a preservative.

225g/8oz poached salmon, boned and cooled
3 anchovy fillets
juice of half a lemon
285g/10oz/2½cups butter
pinch of mace
pinch of ground ginger
salt and freshly ground pepper

1 Pound the salmon with the anchovy fillets, lemon juice and 225g/8oz of the butter until smooth (this is easier and quicker if done in a food processor). Add the mace and ginger and season to taste. Pack the mixture tightly in a suitable pot. Melt the remaining butter and pour over the fish to seal.

Stir-up Sunday

The collect on the Sunday before Advent begins 'Stir up, we beseech thee, O Lord, the wills of thy faithful people; that they, plenteously bringing forth the fruit of good works, may of thee be plenteously rewarded.'

For those whose thoughts centre on their stomachs this prayer acts more as a reminder to stir up less spiritual fruit – Christmas Pudding.

Mixing it is very heavy work and much more fun if it is made into an occasion with all the family taking part. Each person present takes a turn at stirring, using a wooden spoon supposedly in memory of Christ's wooden crib, and, eyes firmly shut, makes a wish while the spoon is dragged laboriously through the dense mixture.

For extra good luck silver charms – coins, a ring and a thimble – are added. On Christmas Day whoever finds a coin will be endowed with worldly fortune, the ring – inevitably – brings marriage and the thimble promises a life of blessedness.

Christmas Pudding

makes 5 x 450g/1lb puddings

This makes a rich, dark and cunningly spiced pudding ripe and ready to eat by Christmas.

225g/8oz/1cup stoned prunes, chopped
225g/8oz/1cup raisins, chopped if desired
225g/8oz/1cup currants, chopped if desired
225g/8oz/1cup sultanas, chopped if desired
225g/8oz/1cup mixed candied peel, chopped
115g/4oz cooking apple, grated
115g/4oz/1cup blanched almonds, chopped
grated zest and juice of 1 orange
grated zest and juice of 1 lemon
225g/8oz/2cups self-raising flour
225g/8oz/1½cups breadcrumbs
225g/8oz/1½cups shredded suet
225g/8oz/1⅓cup soft brown sugar
5ml/1teaspoon mixed spice
5ml/1teaspoon cinnamon
5ml/1teaspoon grated nutmeg
5ml/1teaspoon ground ginger
3 eggs, beaten
300ml/½pint/1¼cups stout
70ml/4tablespoons rum
extra rum for serving

1 Mix together the chopped fruit and nuts and the orange and lemon zest and juices.
2 Sift the flour into a bowl and add the breadcrumbs, suet, sugar and spices.
3 Add the mixed fruits to the bowl and mix thoroughly.
4 Whisk the eggs with the stout and rum. Pour into the mixture, and stir thoroughly until all the ingredients are well blended. This is hard work and could take at least half an hour.

5 Spoon the mixture into greased pudding basins – you will need 5 x 450g/1lb or an equivalent combination – filling them to within 2.5cm/1in of the rim. Cover first with a layer of greaseproof paper and then with a layer of pleated foil, to allow the pudding to rise during cooking. Tie securely with string.

6 Steam the puddings for at least 6 hours; do not forget to top up the pan with boiling water. Remove and store in a cool dry place.

7 On the day, steam the pudding for a further 2–3 hours. Then turn it out and drench it in heated rum. Set it alight and bring to the table where it should be greeted with plenty of ooos and ahhhs of anticipation.

Westmorland Rum Butter

Although usually eaten with Christmas Pudding, this can also be spread on scones, fruit bread and, of course, mince pies. Cumberland butter is made with the same ingredients except for the butter which is melted.

225g/8oz/1cup unsalted butter
450g/1lb/2⅔cups soft brown sugar
5ml/1teaspoon freshly grated nutmeg
70ml/4tablespoons rum

1 Soften the butter by removing it from the fridge and letting it stand for about 30 minutes.
2 Beat in the sugar and nutmeg. Then slowly add the rum.
3 Put it into bowls and leave to set.

Christmas

Nowadays roast turkey with all the trimmings – chipolatas, chestnut stuffing, roast potatoes, Brussels sprouts and bread sauce – is considered the traditional British Christmas meal, but in fact turkey is a relatively recent import from America. Before it arrived we used to tuck into far more exotic fare. At Elizabethan Christmas banquets roast swan was served with side dishes of boar's head, a baron of beef, spiced beef, huge hams and that extra-ordinary culinary feat of a boned goose stuffed with a boned capon, stuffed with a boned pheasant, stuffed with a boned partridge, stuffed with a boned quail stuffed with sweetmeats.

Mince pies have also changed. Once they were eaten before the meal and made from real mincemeat – often fat mutton – baked with fruit and spices in cases to represent Christ's manger. Even Christmas Pudding is not the same: in medieval times it was known as Plum Porridge or Pottage and made with beef and veal stewed with prunes, currants and raisins, spices, sugar, sack (a once popular wine from the Canary Isles and similar to sherry), lemon juice and claret, but by the nineteenth century the meat had been dropped and it became more like our modern day version.

Baked Ham

Many households still sport a baked ham on the bone on their Christmas sideboards, festively dressed in a paper ruffle. Some hams, especially if they are dry-cured, need to be soaked overnight in water otherwise they taste too salty. The most effective way of baking a ham is to wrap it up in a 'huff', a flour and water paste, which seals in all the juices and prevents it from drying out. Do remember that once all the meat has been carved, the bone can be used to make a superb split-pea soup.

5.5–6.5kg/12–14lb ham
1.35kg/3lb plain flour
850ml/1½pints/3¾cups water
cloves

1 Soak the ham overnight in cold water. The next day drain the ham and dry it thoroughly.
2 Mix the flour with enough of the water to make a stiff paste, roll out the paste and wrap it around the ham, pinching the edges together tightly and sealing them with a little water.
3 Bake the ham in a preheated 180°C/350°F/gas4 oven, allowing about 25 minutes per 450g/lb.
4 Remove the ham from the oven and break the huff. Lift out the ham and leave to cool for about 5 minutes. Then peel off the skin – you can usually just pull it off with your hands – and trim the fat. With a sharp knife score the fat crossways into a diamond pattern and stud the centre of each diamond with a clove.
5 Brush the ham all over with the glaze of your choice (see below) or, if you are using breadcrumbs, press them into the fat. Turn up the oven to 190°C/375°F/gas5 and roast the ham for 30 minutes.

Marmalade glaze
75ml/5tablespoons/⅓cup marmalade
20ml/1tablespoon/1½tablespoons whisky

Mix together and spread over the ham.

Mustard glaze
50ml/3tablespoons/¼cup clear honey
50ml/3tablespoons/¼cup English mustard powder
salt and freshly ground black pepper

Melt the honey and stir in the mustard. Season and
spread all over the ham.

Breadcrumbs
450g/1lb/4cups dry breadcrumbs
5ml/1teaspoon finely chopped parsley
salt and freshly ground black pepper

Mix the ingredients together and press them firmly
into the ham's layer of fat. This is best done while
the meat is still warm.

Cumberland Sauce

Serve either hot or cold with the ham.

150ml/¼pint/⅔cup ruby port
juice and grated zest of 1 orange
225g/8oz redcurrant jelly
5ml/1teaspoon mustard powder
salt and freshly ground black pepper

1 Simmer the port and orange zest for 2–3 minutes, stir in the redcurrant jelly and simmer for a further couple of minutes until it has melted.
2 Mix together the orange juice and mustard powder and add to the redcurrant mixture. Season and simmer for about 2–3 minutes.

Pickled Pears

6 large ripe pears, peeled, cored and sliced
450g/1lb/2cups sugar
250ml/⅓pint/1cup red wine vinegar
1 cinnamon stick
10 cloves
5ml/1teaspoon allspice
5ml/1teaspoon nutmeg

1 Put the pears in a saucepan, add enough water to cover the pears and bring to the boil. After 5 minutes stir in the sugar and vinegar and then add the cinnamon stick, cloves, allspice and nutmeg. Simmer for about 25 minutes, then remove from the heat and leave to cool overnight.
2 The following morning, drain the pears and pack into sterilized jars. Boil the cooking liquor to reduce by about one third and pour over the pears. Seal while warm and keep for at least one month before eating to allow the flavours to mellow.

Wassailing

Here we come a-wassailing
Among the leaves so green,
And here we come a-wandering
So fair to be seen:

Love and joy come to you,
And to you your wassail too,
And God bless you, and send you
A Happy New Year.
And God send you a Happy New Year.

At one time in England and Wales most houses kept a wassail bowl ready throughout the Christmas festivities for unexpected guests. Carol singers carried their own cups to dip into the drink after they had sung.

Wassail comes from Old English 'wes hal', meaning 'be thou whole', and drinking from the wassail bowl was an expression of friendship; the custom of drinking your neighbours' good health probably came to be called toasting after the 'sippets' or pieces of toast floating in the wassail bowl.

Even the apple trees were wassailed to ensure a good crop. In Devon, on twelfth night, some farmers and their families still gather around the trees with shotguns or pots and pans. They make a tremendous noise to raise the Sleeping Tree Spirit and to scare off the demons. Then a toast is drunk and, for extra luck, some of the branches are dipped into the wassail bowl.

Wassail Cup

serves 8

8 small eating apples
32 cloves
1.5litres/2½pints/6¼cups brown ale
300ml/½pint/1¼cups sweet sherry
pinch of ground cinnamon
pinch of ground ginger
pinch of ground nutmeg
grated zest of 1 lemon
2 slices bread, toasted

1 Slit the skin around the centre of the apples and stud them with cloves. Put them in a baking tin with 150ml/¼pint/⅔cup of the brown ale and bake in a 200°C/400°F/gas6 oven for about 30 minutes, basting occasionally.
2 Heat the remaining brown ale with the sherry, spices and lemon zest and simmer for about 5 minutes.
3 Cut the toast and the baked apples into small pieces, and serve the punch very hot, in a punch bowl, with the pieces floating on top.